100%

JOB INTERVIEW

SUCCESS

100%
JOB INTERVIEW
SUCCESS

How To Always Succeed
At Job Interviews

By Marricke Kofi GANE

Contents

INTRODUCTION vii

1 ATTENDING AN INTERVIEW - THE BASICS 1

2 WHAT ARE YOU BRINGING TO
   THIS ORGANISATION? 17

3 HOW DID YOU FIND OUT ABOUT THIS JOB? 21

4 HOW LONG WERE YOU IN YOUR LAST JOB FOR? 25

5 WHY DO YOU WANT TO WORK
   FOR THIS ORGANISATION? 29

6 WHERE DO YOU SEE YOURSELF IN "X" YEARS? 33

7 OTHER QUESTIONS FROM EMPLOYERS 35

8 20 THINGS YOU SHOULD NEVER DO
   AT JOB INTERVIEWS? 39

   AUTHOR'S OTHER WORKS 49

   ABOUT THE AUTHOR 53

INTRODUCTION

This is a no-nonsense guide to passing your interviews. I needed to get that out of the way. I have read quite a number of interview books – most so large and complicated that by the time you have finished reading them, you are more confused going into the interview than you were when you clicked "buy" on the Amazon marketplace. Others go as far as trying to change you, in the short time you have available, by trying to teach you new psychological techniques, some of which require a great deal of practice to master. If those are factors you are seeking, then this book is certainly not for you. This book is sweet, short and simple. It focuses directly on the points you need to quickly absorb in the shortest possible time for your interview. Now that we are on the same page, let's continue.

With redundancies becoming more common place and with people now being able to work remotely across the globe and from home, it is becoming clearer by the day that the competition surrounding each job opening today is greater than existed many years ago. Sadly with the advent and increasing complexity of technology, this trend will not evaporate, but rather increase. What does that mean for you? Simple – it means if you ever get a shot at an interview, psyche yourself mentally. It may be the only interview opportunity you will receive for a long time and as such, you need to throw everything at it to land the job, first time.

It is reasonable to assume that IF you are called for an interview, your qualifications as shown on your CV, have won you half a place already. We would assume therefore that you know your "content" or that you are at least knowledgeable in the area being recruited for. The rest, which usually is a face to face interview, is up to you to impress at – and this is where this short and sweet guide comes into play. Whisper this to yourself the whole time you are seated in that interview room – "I haven't come this far to fail this interview."

Passing job interviews has very little to do with luck. If you know how, you can always bring yourself to be in the top three ranked candidates at the end of every interview – and that, will definitely increase your chances of getting "your" choice of jobs every time.

The three most important things you need to know about are the organisation you are applying to work for, the job being offered and yourself. Interestingly, you don't need to know everything about these three – but you do need to know the most relevant and important things. In this little book, I'll show you exactly what to look out for, so that you don't waste your time hunting for unnecessary information which will eventually ruin your chances of success. In fact I will even teach you how to answer some very key interview questions – those that can make or break your chances of success. Besides all these, I'll give you a treasure you won't get anywhere else – I will show you how employers are thinking when they ask you certain questions, what their expectations are, how they interpret your answers and more.

After reading this guide, you will walk into your next interview(s) not only knowing what do to before the interview starts, but also understanding how to answer the tough questions correctly. You'll go in knowing exactly how your interviewer(s) think and how to make them happy with your performance.

Now, get your confidence boosted – go get that job you've always wanted.

1

ATTENDING AN INTERVIEW - THE BASICS

The important thing to do with any job interview is to research the organisation thoroughly. After all, this is where you are going to be committing half the waking hours of your life for five out of seven days a week for the next two or more years. Most importantly, try and understand what they do as an organisation and precisely what you will be required to do when you are accepted for the job. I have seen many candidates who don't do any research or who wait until the day of the interview before asking questions. If this is your attitude to interviews then I would like to politely say that you already have a 90% chance of failure at the interview. If you have already been failing at interviews, you probably have just discovered one of the reasons why. For starters, there are some very, very basic things you should note which can increase your chances of success:

If Looks Could Kill – Don't Kill The Interviewer, Kill The Competition

Always dress smartly – a suit, a shirt or other suitable clothing makes you look attractively welcoming. Don't listen to rumour – don't be deceived that some job interviews don't really require you to "dress suitably." It really is better to dress adequately than to end up looking like the odd one out – nobody will be employing anyone who can't be bothered to make a first decent impression. The truth is, it may be the only impression you'll get the chance to make, so make it count. If it turns out that your dress code is not a priority consideration, you won't lose anything, but if the reverse were true, you would be kicking yourself.

I advise that moderate is good – This means that for men avoid the shiny suit, the overly bright coloured shirt, the skin tight trousers and the bling watch – unless the role is for a catwalk model, leave that style for the carnival. For women, the interview day is not one for your highest heels, the most talked-about hairstyle, excessively long nails or hazard-light lip colouring. Effectively all I am saying is that on the interview day there are really just two parts of your body which need to be well dressed up – your face, with a smile, and your brains with insights. Beyond that, everything else should be labelled as "moderate."

Time Is Not Just Money; Time Is Winning

Always try to arrive at least 15 minutes early. It simply tells whether you are serious about getting the job or not. If you have to travel, factor in an extra 30 – 45 minutes for any eventuality you may encounter on the way. Don't worry if you arrive too early. It will simply make you more relaxed about the interview or prove to your prospective employer that you are more serious about getting the job than other candidates. And whilst waiting, smile and be courteous to everybody – you never know who may be stamping you as "HIRED" even before you step into the interview. If you have time at the reception, grab any material available in the waiting area which has been produced by the company. You will be amazed at the useful and informative things contained find in it.

This Failure Is Due To Technical Problems Within Your Control

Always remember to turn your phone off as soon as you arrive at the interview venue. Don't forget this. You have no excuse if your phone rings during an interview. This is as good as losing half the marks before you even started. You will be surprised at this, but it's true – phones have a knack for ringing in situations where it would cause you the most embarrassment.

Don't Go To A Round Hole, If You Are A Square Peg

Always obtain a job specification, job description or go through the vacancy details thoroughly. Be sure you completely understand what they expect you to deliver to the organisation when you are employed. You could be asked a surprise question on the "Job Description" and if you do not have the answer ready to hand, the interview could end right there. Think about it – if you don't thoroughly understand what you will be required to do when you are employed, the chances are that you will either be doing nothing or doing wrong things wrong should the job be given you. The other immediate interpretation this could spell out is this – if you don't thoroughly understand what is going to be required of you in the job, the chances are that you have not assessed whether or not you have the skills and knowledge to get it done in the first place. Now that is not to say that your ability to fit into every requirement of the job is the most crucial thing. Employers understand that a new job is like a pair of shoes – if the fit is too tight, the chances are that your skills and experience will continue to grow and very soon outgrow the role – similarly to your feet outgrowing your shoes. You should be able to demonstrate that aside from fitting most of the requirements of the role, it also presents opportunities for you to expand your skills and knowledge in areas where you were previously limited.

You see, employers know that if a role and a candidate together produce a win-win scenario for each other, then the chances are that the potential employee will stay longer or at least enjoy the role. Most candidates however go into interviews making it appear like they have everything to give to the role, but the role has no value to add to them. Well, in that case, the most relevant question any sensible employer will ask is "What happens after you've given all you know to the role, what then?" Sadly, that may be the only question they don't openly ask you and sadly, it would be the one that requires your answer the most.

Everybody Likes To Be Understood – Even Your Potential Employer

Always make time to read the organisation's website and especially anything about them in the news. I would usually suggest that you look for the organisation's most recent mention in the media (most organisations will have links of this on their website) and once found, try to locate what it is about that media coverage that relates closely to the area or department you are being recruited into. For example, if you just read a media report about a new contract the company has just won and you are about to be recruited into the HR department, you need to imme-diately start asking how that news will impact on the HR unit you are being recruited into. Is it a specialist contract that is likely to require the recruitment of specialist staff and which is new to HR? Is the new contract likely to see a surge in employee numbers therefore meaning you will be thrown into a busy period in HR's history?

No employer likes being "patronised" – you must make an effort to read and know enough about the entity you'll be spending more than 40% of your daily life serving. This is very useful when you get asked questions like "What do you know about this organisation? You will be saying something relevant and beyond that, something which you can directly connect to the relevance of the department you are being recruited into – now that should impress a potential employer. Otherwise it shows your lack of commitment even before it is required of you. To any employer, any uncommitted employee is regarded as not having the best interests of the organisation to heart and as such, is most likely not to care whether the organisation fails or succeeds.

Look out for little things about the company which other companies don't do – every employer will be impressed to see that you know what sets them apart. It will set you apart in their minds. If you are being employed as an accountant for example, look at their latest Annual Audited Accounts – see what you can find in it that sets it apart from other companies. If you are to be employed as an HR personnel, look at their retention level or a graduate trainee scheme they run which other companies in their industry don't run. Always look out for something about the potential employer which directly relates to the unit you are being recruited into and which sets the company apart from others.

All Employers Are Born Equal, To Become Different

Always research and remember three key aspects of the organisation which makes them stand out. To make it even more effective, I suggest that the peculiarities you choose to remember are those which knit very closely with the department you are hoping to be recruited into. As I said earlier, most organisations are formed because they have something different to offer than their competitors. Throughout the life of companies therefore, they try as much as is practical, to continue differentiating themselves. It's what makes them unique in every way and it is therefore easy to warm the hearts of your interviewers by showing that you understand what makes them different. It immediately projects you as someone who is different enough to be a part of their organisation. If you have friends or colleagues already in the organisation, question them specifically on what they feel makes their employer different – there are some organisational cultures that will never be known by outsiders, but which potentially sets an organisation apart. Knowing these internal cultures can be subconscious indications to the interviewer(s) that you know enough to be a part of their corporate family.

Know A "Smartie" By His Questions And A Fool, By His Rants

Always prepare three questions to ask at the end of the interview. For example, what will be your expectations of me in my first month of employment? What is it like working for this organisation? What is the next big direction for this organisation?" Most candidates think asking questions at the end of an interview is not needed. Well, it could also be interpreted as "You are not interested enough to want to know more about your potential employer." Here is what you should know: You don't know "everything" about your potential employer even if you've researched it very thoroughly or asked questions of people already working in it. By saying you don't have any questions to ask merely portrays one of two things (a) you are a pretender, pretending to know everything (b) you just want the job and you don't want to know anything more about the organisation. Asking a question can also be a way of revealing how intelligent you are. It doesn't have to be a question which generates an international debate or one that makes the interviewers feel "incapable" but simply a question which portrays that you really do want to understand what it is you are getting into.

Diplomatic Immunity Against Etiquette Violations

Always wait to be offered a seat before you seat down – it portrays your respect for the interviewer and your understanding of etiquette. When you do, mirror your interviewers. This book may not offer the platform to explain how mirrored behaviours work, but it is enough to understand that scientific research proves that it is a psychological behaviour which consistently succeeds. Now without getting into the complexities of it, all I want to recommend is that the more you mirror the physical stance of your interviewer, the more it registers on their subconscious minds (quite involuntarily), that you are connecting with them. So if s/he crosses their legs, find a sly way of crossing yours without them noticing. However, bear in mind to do only what is reasonable as one being interviewed.

Connect And Stay Connected Throughout

Smile and give lots of eye contact with everybody present on the panel, not just the one asking the question. Many people miss this – if you are at an interview with more than one interviewer, note that the one asking all the questions may not necessarily be the one who has a final authority to hire you. Eye contact demonstrates acknowledgement and respect for the people present. Yes, upbringing in certain cultures (I personally have this experience) trains us to believe that looking into someone's eyes whilst they talk to you equates to disrespect. In the corporate world however, that may be viewed as the direct opposite and to your disadvantage. It may be interpreted as meaning you have something to hide or you are not speaking the truth. So, I suggest if that is your cultural upbringing, then for once, and for the purposes of your job interview alone, break that cultural law – and do your best to unlearn it subsequently. If keeping eye contact still appears difficult for you, then use a simple trick which most great public speakers use. Look either in the space between their eyes or at the very top of their heads or foreheads – it still appears to them as though you were looking them in the eyes. So at least you have the desired effect needed, but without cultural discomfort to you.

Mirrors Don't Lie; Energy Reflects Energy – Always

Always sit up straight and be enthusiastic with your answers and questions - don't speak in an undertone or drag your voice. This coupled with slumping in your chair can communicate many negative things. It could be interpreted as the interviewers being boring; you are disinterested in the interview process; that you will be reflecting the same attitude in the role should you get hired; you are passive and won't add any energy or value to the organ-isation or that you simply lack confidence for the role. Remember, the energy you show will eventually reflect in the enthusiasm to hire you. Nobody wants a "kill-joy" – naturally, people with energy are inspiring. Don't be surprised - your energy may be the very helping hand of inspiration to lift an interviewer from their current rather lowly state – and what better way to demonstrate their being drawn to you, than to feel happy giving you the role?

And Finally.....

People say to me that the culture of nepotism *(the "who-you-know" factor)* in play during recruitments can be a very high determinant in some places – I don't deny it exists. But I also believe very genuinely *(because I have also experienced it)* that if you do your homework well, and perform exceptionally well, in fact so well that your potential employer knows that you have proven yourself beyond a doubt as the best and most suited candidate for the role – it will be very, very difficult to exercise nepotism on their part. Even if they did, at least their sleep wouldn't be so sweet where you are concerned. Besides, you can at least hold your head up high.

In terms of interview questions, the easiest and most practical way I have found around preparing for them is to do this - draw a table with two columns and as many rows. In the first column list down all the most important things (businesses/activities) the organisation does and also the job requirements (i.e. the actual activities or duties that you will be required to do in this role if you are accepted) For example, filing customer applications orderly on a daily basis, preparing a bank reconciliation statement at the end of every month, chasing up customers for unpaid loans etc). In the other column, try and match line by line, writing down every activity, experience, skills or anything you have done before or are still doing, that makes it possible for you to contribute to or perform the particular business activity or job requirement respectively on each line. Hopefully by the end of this exercise, you should also be able to figure out if you are (by your own assessment) suited for the role.

Job Requirements/ Organisation's Operations	Why I Fit / How I can Add Value
Company is looking to venture into Oil and Gas Funding	My Master's Dissertation (published) focused on new funding techniques for the oil sector with startling empirical results. I can add value by bring my thorough research into the process of helping the organisation determine the best funding tools to deploy.

Job requires negotiation skills	I haven't negotiated in the oil Sector, but have negotiated and succeeded in sealing four nego-tiations with VPt Bank over 3 years. None of which were below $ 'X million (example)

Let me just say however, that most people's understanding when it comes to the word *"experience"* has to change a little, otherwise, you may wrongfully write yourself off as inexperienced for a lot of jobs. There is such a thing as *"transferrable skills."* So although you may be applying for say a job in banking and finance, there may be many things in the job description you could do (without further training) as a result of a remotely similar activity you may have done in your old job in a manufacturing company or even at school, even if you have never worked in the banking and finance sector before. Experience (as most people see it) doesn't necessarily mean it must be exactly the same as described in the job requirement or in the same and exact industry or country or level. Experience should be understood on the basis of "Does a task I have experienced doing, make me very capable of delivering on the requirements of this current role I am applying for?

In the following very short chapters, we delve into some very common questions arising during interviews. It is interesting to note that in spite of all the advancement in psychometric testing and other scientific approaches to interviewing, these are questions most employers still want to ask and hear answers to. We will explore how they should be understood, both by the candidate and from the perspective of the interviewer.

2

WHAT ARE YOU
BRINGING TO THIS
ORGANISATION?

From The Perspective Of The Candidate

The easiest way to prepare for this sort of question is to research and find out where the organisation is trying to go, where they are heading, their plans for the future and what they say they need to do to get there. Which new activities, business operations, new products, new systems are coming on board? Then ask yourself, which skills or knowledge do you have, needed by the organisation, to reach those goals? All employers are happy to have employees whose skills or knowledge will help the organisation move into the future. Understand that it's not all about skill – It's also about relevant, usable, progressive knowledge.

If you are just graduating from university or hold a professional qualification, you may not have a skill but more crucially, a certain new knowledge that will be a useful ingredient in the potential employer's future operations – this is your ace card, use it. So remember: Try matching the future direction of the organisation with the skills or knowledge you have which may be good ingredients for that direction – that is what you are bringing to the organisation; an ingredient for their present or future success. It's a subtle way of saying that you understand that the organisation needs to move forward, you have a fair idea where it is moving and what is needed to get there and that you have "SOME" of the needed inputs to get it there – that's progressive recruitment.

From The Perspective Of The Employer

This is the one question that will make a lot of candidates feel deflated or defeated. Interestingly however, it is the one question which enables interviewers to see the candidate's confidence and his/her ability to demonstrate a clear understanding of who s/he believes the potential employer is looking for in the role. When the interviewer starts hearing generic answers like *"I am hardworking"* or *"I am a team player"* etc., they will soon recognise the candidate either doesn't know what it is the organisation is looking for, or hasn't carefully assessed what s/he is capable of offering the role, should they get it. It is a question which will also test the candidate's ability to demonstrate that their past experiences are usable in the organisation's current state, or if s/he is dynamic and understands trends in business. They may further highlight their skills, experiences etc. which may not be useful now but soon will be in the future.

Finally, it tells the interviewer point-blank if the candidate can "sell" convincingly. Being able to sell is entirely different from being a sales person. If you can sell yourself, you can sell anything. It also shows persuasion skills. And don't be fooled – employers know that business is really all about selling – everybody is selling, from the shop floor person trying to convince customers to buy the company's products or services to the chief executive trying to convince the entire organisation that his new direction will work, given the support.

3

HOW DID YOU FIND OUT ABOUT THIS JOB?

From The Perspective Of The Candidate

This is one of those questions you really can't lie about, but my suggestion is that if it is possible, decide where you want your career to go. Is it auditing, accountancy, consultancy, banking, human resource, development, training etc? Once you have determined that, start looking for jobs in the right places. Employers who want the best HR personnel are more likely to advertise excellent positions in magazines, websites or similar platforms which are subscribed to by HR enthusiasts. The same applies to other career paths. For some employers, potential employees who read their adverts on these types of platforms appear to them as being more focused and more discerning. They appear to potential employers as people who know where to look for the right things. However, where these kinds of targeted newsletters, magazines, internet sites or platforms don't exist in your particular country, don't worry, this question won't be taking too many marks away from you. The other angle to it is this – if you heard about the role from a friend, colleague, family, etc –there is a high chance that you are the kind of person with good human relations and therefore you are good at keeping and managing your contacts – this is a superior skill for any employee to have.

From The Perspective Of The Employer

This question is quite deceptive. To the candidate, it is a straightforward question and nothing to lie about (no sense in doing so), but to the interviewer it provides tremendous insight, depending also on where an advert was placed. A candidate who learnt about the job by word of mouth in social circles or through colleagues is likely to be considered by the employer as having strong relationship building skills. Learning about the job from a niche publication such as an industry specific magazine rather than a widely public newspaper may indicate that s/he is very discerning or focused. On the other hand any indication that the job was referred to the candidate by someone in the organisation is likely to mean that they have already been investigating the organisation or at least have been talking to someone about it.

4

HOW LONG WERE YOU
IN YOUR LAST JOB FOR?

From The Perspective Of The Candidate

Here again, employers want to separate out those who are unstable from those who are. If you are always leaving jobs within or up to a year, you are likely to be considered as very unstable. You need to understand the way employers think. Most of them take employees on, use about six or so months to teach them about their companies and how things are done, and remember they will be spending money on you all this time. So if you leave within another six months, they have just made a loss. Now, potential employers don't have a way of gauging how long you will stay with them except by looking at how long you have stayed in other places. If you are just seeking a job for the first time or you have left a few places in the past within one year, then you'll need to provide some assurance to the potential employer that you don't intend to leave their employment anytime soon. You can't just say "I'll be here for a while" – you have to let them see a reason why you intend to stay. Maybe you have a personal programme to gain as much experience from this particular employer that you can't find with any organisation (and don't try to flatter them, because they always know); maybe the organisation itself provides an excellent personnel development programme that you want to take full advantage of; maybe you are a family person and you need some stability in your career; maybe you have gained a great deal of experience in other places and now, you need to settle down; maybe they are the only organisation which provides the type of career you want to develop in; or maybe you have other past events in your life that you can use to prove that you are a very committed person (not your girlfriend/boyfriend type of commitment though). Whatever the case give the potential employer a reason to believe s/he won't be making a loss employing you.

From The Perspective Of The Employer

Employers will always draw a conclusion from this question by looking at two things; first, the frequency and second, the reason. If the candidate has left all their previous jobs in less than two years and mostly because of conflict with someone, then surely employers need to ask more questions because, all those people can't be so impossible to work with. It is also a question for which the employer is highly likely to request specific answers to his/her questions and not the general well-known answers such as; "I was looking for better opportunities" – well then, what opportunities were you looking for that your former employer didn't provide?

5

WHY DO YOU WANT TO WORK FOR THIS ORGANISATION?

From The Perspective Of The Candidate

STOP! Don't open your mouth if what you are about to say is very generic. For example, things like because you treat your staff well, because you are the leader in the industry; because you are the biggest company. STOP IT! This is the one question that shows clearly, which candidates have thoroughly researched the organisation BUT most importantly who know by themselves whether this is the right company for them or not.

Here is what you should also know – this question is also an opportunity for you to demonstrate to your employer that you are different from everybody else, because the truth is – everybody else is likely to be giving those same generic answers. What the employer is trying to establish with this question is whether or not the organisation also satisfies any of your needs or expectations. This is based on the understanding that no two people can agree to be together, and be successful in doing, except if they are satisfied with each other – in other words, the organisation must be happy that you'll satisfy its expectations and you, on the other hand must also be satisfied that the organisation will satisfy your expectations. Most jobseekers don't recognise the latter, but it is very true.

So how do you prepare for this kind of question? Make a list of the things that would make any job, your most satisfying job (I said satisfying NOT perfect) Also list down your future career plans, professional plans, development plans, personal plans that are closely related to your career. Now, find out by researching, if there are things about and within the organisation that will satisfy the needs and expectations you listed. I'm hoping you wouldn't see this as just a step to getting a job but it should also help you determine whether this is an employment you will be happy in or not. If anything about the organisation (now or its future) conflicts in a major way with your current or future plans, think twice.

From The Perspective Of The Employer

This question helps the employer pick up a few things. Firstly whether the candidate, by his or herself has assessed the culture of the organisation as matching their personal culture, and the reason the candidate really wants to be there. It will also tell you whether they have done any work in trying to understand the organisation or if they are just looking for somewhere to work for now. By asking this question the employer will also be able to find out the areas and parameters on which the candidates feel connected to the organisation? If any of those parameters happen to be the organisation's top cultures or values or principles, then, with some degree of certainty, the candidate will feel more at home there.

6

WHERE DO YOU SEE YOURSELF IN "X" YEARS?

From The Perspective Of The Candidate

This is quite a straightforward question. Nobody knows your future plans like you do. The employer is only trying to see whether your future plans will at any time conflict with their plans – because if they do, you are most likely to leave the organisation. It doesn't mean however, that you have to change your plans. If you want to increase your chances on this question do this: Find out what the future plans of the organisation are and also what it is currently doing on a day to day basis. Now figure out what your future plans are for the next three years. Ask yourself one by one 'If the company did "X" today or "Y" in the future, would it hinder me from achieving item "Z" on my list of plans?' If the plans of the organisation and its activities today or in the future will affect you in any way, then you need to be thinking twice what you are getting yourself into – one way or another, it will be obvious to a smart interviewer.

From The Perspective Of The Employer

This question should really answer two concerns for any employer – (a) is the candidate likely to stick around in employment long enough for them to recoup their initial investment in the candidate? (b) Is the employer's organisation in the picture of the candidate's future, and if not, what should be done? Employers have the unique advantage of knowing what the organisation's plan for the future are; the candidate doesn't. For this reason, it is easier for an employer to take whatever the candidate says and assess it side by side the employer's plans for the next five years – are they parallel or crossing paths?

7

OTHER QUESTIONS
FROM EMPLOYERS

"What Has Been Your Most Recent Achievement And When Was It?"

Achievers (if they ever become achievers) live literally on achievements, no matter how big or small. That's how you tell the difference between those who merely claim to be achievers and those who are actual achievers – the latter always have something to back it. There's another angle to it – whether big or small, achievers still recognise what an achievement is. Non-achievers on the other hand, even when they do achieve, don't recognise it as such. Every organisation sets out to be successful and to accumulate achievements. If such an organisation is intent on continuing in its success, it will do the wise thing of making success and achievement part of its culture.

"What Was The Last Thing You Failed In And How Did You Take It?"

A fact about business is that things don't always go as planned – not always. Unfortunately however, not everybody can deal with failure. And for people like that, it not only takes a long while to shake off the failure and move on to the next stage (mind you, business doesn't sit and wait for one to recover), it is also contagious. With this question, an employer can attempt to peek into the candidate's tendency towards failure – do they learn their lesson from the failure, dust themselves down and face the next music, or do they lie there in the mud of failure, throw a tantrum and pull everybody else with them into the mud? The question also gives some insight into the candidate's attitude to risk. Is s/he a risk taker at all? S/he doesn't need to be the type who is happy taking all the risk in the world (that in itself is very dangerous) but they must at least appear to be willing to take some risk. If not, you can be sure s/he is not the kind of candidate you should expect to help the organisation find, explore or try new opportunities.

The following questions are also commonly asked at interviews. The key to answering them is to think about HOW, WHY, WHEN and the OUTCOME. Try to give specific examples from where you have worked, during your education or from extra-curricular activities.

Initiative:-

Share an incidence that required you to utilise your initiative, what did you do and what was the result?

Dealing with a difficult boss/team member:-

Have you had to deal with difficult people in the past – how did you go about it and what was the result?

Team Working:-

What would you do if a team you were part of was not working well together?

Prioritising:-

If three people came to you with work, all saying that their work was important, how would you prioritise?

Organisation:-

Give us an example of an incident in which you had to demonstrate your organisational skill

Deadlines:-

Has there ever been an incident when you didn't meet a deadline? Why and what would you do differently?

Implementing new systems-

Have you ever implemented a new system? If so what did you do, why and what was the result?

Dealing with people:-

How would you deal with a Chief Executive? Would this differ from how you would deal with a junior, and if so why?

Flexibility:-

Give us an example of how you have demonstrated flexibility in the past?

8

20 THINGS YOU SHOULD NEVER DO AT JOB INTERVIEWS?

This may definitely not be a conclusive list, but I feel they are things not to lose sight of during an interview process.

1. Turning Up Late

This should not happen in the first place which is why you don't need to take the chance. Set off very early. Its irritating how, only on the day of your interview that traffic and everything else seems to work against you. If it happens, you had better have such a reasonable excuse that it cannot be ignored. And at every opportunity, call in and let the interviewer know.

2. Fidgeting With Unnecessary Props

Please! Please! Please! Find a very diplomatic way of hiding your nerves and fears. Don't fidget with the pen, the books, folders, mobile phone, nails, your thigh or beard - don't do it. It sends too many wrong messages. For example that you may be lying about something, or that you are not confident you can settle in the role, etc.

3. Unclear Answering And Rambling

If you don't know the answer to a question, say so and with a "sorry," but don't rant something totally off track. It isn't really the time to fool your way out. It can make the interviewer feel his/her intelligence is being insulted. And don't mumble. If the interviewer(s) has to ask what you just said more than three times, then you will start to lose it all on their score-sheet.

4. Speaking Negatively About Your Current Employer

If you don't have anything good to say about your former employer(s), please don't say anything. It won't go well for you if you do. The potential employer is likely to see himself in the same position when you finally leave their employment.

5. Lying On Your CV

Don't for one minute think that your CV (which the interviewer has in front of him) has been sent to the potential employer and as such, you won't be asked about it – Wrong. Some interviewers will actually ask you to go through your CV – It would be unfortunate for you to start fabricating or not know the details of the jobs or roles that you have on your CV. Once inconsistencies start appearing between what your CV says and what you are saying, nothing you are likely to say from that point onwards is likely to be received as convincing by the panel.

6. Getting Personal Or Too Familiar

As far as possible, please avoid flirting with any of the interviewers, even if you know them. DON'T start putting across personal emotionally charged stories as the reasons why you need the job. If you start giving personal reasons such as having been unemployed for a while, family bills to pay, indebtedness etc for wanting the job, any smart employer would ask themselves "And once you get the job and these problems are no more, then what?

7. Discussing Money Or Time Off

Unless it is put on the table by the interviewer, avoid as far as possible talking about salary packages, sick and holiday leave, or welfare policies. It soon becomes obvious you are not attending the interview for anything other than for money and people with that kind of dispensation hardly add any value to any role – they simply take!

8. Cursing

You don't have to be told this, but no matter how cool you think it makes you feel, using foul and inappropriate language is generally not acceptable at any time in the workplace, let alone at an interview which will determine if you'll get the job in the first place.

9. Not Following Up

This is something not many candidates do after an interview – so the few that do it get an extra advantage. Even if you think your performance at the interview wasn't that great, you should still send the potential employer a short email message to say thank you for the opportunity and that you are still very enthusiastic about getting the job. Don't leave it days after the interview – do it the same day of the interview. The little extra effort only goes to show that you are a cut more serious about the role than all the others.

10. Don't Use Clichés

Keep this in mind – you are unlikely to be the first candidate most of the panel are seeing in their career lifetime. The truth is they've probably heard all the clichés they can hear at an interview. You have a choice to also use them and be lumped with every other candidate or to differentiate yourself and go straight to the top of the list: Find other ways of saying it, but don't use clichés like: "I'm a problem-solver." "I'm a real team player." "I'm a perfectionist." Give specific occurrences or examples to clarify your points.

11. Don't Be Evasive

Direct questions will demand direct answers. In fact at an interview, assume every questions demand direct answers. Once you start detracting from the core answer your nerves will start reflecting the psyche with which you are giving the answers. Whether you are lying or telling the truth, your voice tone and body language will reflect the same. Truth is, you can fool some people sometimes, but you can't fool your body language all the time

12. Don't Just Walk Away

Usually when the interview is about to end, after all the questions you will normally be asked if there are any final comments you'd like to make. Take this opportunity to reiterate that you really see yourself fitting in the job and that you really do want it. Then you can ask the interview panel when they are likely to get back to you with a decision or interest. Whatever you do, DON'T just say "thank you" and walk away.

13. Don't Be Arrogant

Knowing within yourself that you have answers to all the questions being asked and being happy with it should not make you come across as arrogant. Don't start speaking or behaving like you've already got the job – you might be unpleasantly surprised. It will be far more profitable to your chances if you keep calm throughout the interview. If you know something that a panellist or interviewer doesn't know, control yourself. Don't let it show on the large screen of your ego. Nothing puts off a potential employer than an arrogant candidate – from the point it is first exhibited, most interviewers simply shut down from listening to you any further.

14. Keep Away From Some Topics

The fact that some interviewers may have decided to ease the rules a little in order to create a friendlier, rather than strict bureaucratic atmosphere does not mean every topic is reasonable to bring up during the interview. It is more sensitive to talk about certain topics than it is others. I suggest as much as possible, avoid the topics of religion, politics and gender relations.

15. No Notes, Means, No Notes

Don't read from notes or your CV — you should be familiar enough with your own history to be able to talk about it unprompted.

16. Don't Argue With Your Prospective Boss

No matter the provocation, whether intended or unintended, avoid getting into ANY form of argument with any of your interviewers. You are the one guaranteed to lose in the end.

17. If You Talk Too Much

If the interviewer has to ask you to stop running your mouth more than once and had to make an effort to get your attention before s/he even put her question or clarification across to you, you have a big problem on your hands – For one, it shows you have no listening or moderation skills. Quite simply, if you can't listen during the interview, chances are that you won't be able to listen or take instructions on the job and that could cost the organisation – employees who don't listen to anyone but themselves.

18. If You Don't Talk Enough

Keep it moderate. I know there are a few out there who are very introverted, but that's no excuse during an interview to have the interviewer beg answers out of you. Just like in the case of talking too much above – it makes it hard to communicate. Again, putting it simple: communication is the lifeblood in any relationship. If you don't talk just enough, any good employer can foresee that there will be a problem with you communicating with others within the organisation – and that can make things go very, very wrong.

19. Speak The Facts Only When You Know The Facts

In the world today, information and knowledge quite easily abound. What we call "facts" have various and many matrixes which determine why one fact is considered more authoritative then others – one of which is the source of the stated fact. If you are going in for an interview and you feel there will be the need to mention some facts, it is essential that you do not offer such facts at random, with any source backing. Again, remember anybody on the panel could have easily researched your facts too, so you getting it all wrong can cost you.

20. Don't Turn The Weakness Question
Into A Positive

When interviewers ask about your weaknesses, they know we all have a few, so it's quite insulting of their intelligence if you try to paint yourself as someone without any. Instead, I suggest to think about a weakness that can be improved, but which does not impact on any of the core requirements of the job you are applying for.

AUTHOR'S OTHER WORKS

Title: Is This Why Africa Is? (E-book & Paperback)
Description: I ask all the questions about Africa that nobody
else will. Deep, profound questions
Availability: Amazon & Kindle
Link to View: http://goo.gl/ecRMig

Title: Where Did God Hide His Diamonds?
(E-book & Paperback)
Description: Discovering what exactly God has hidden in you,
finding it & prospering freely from it
Availability: Amazon & Kindle
Link to View: http://goo.gl/ecRMig

Title: Doing Business with God (E-book & Paperback)
Description: 60 shocking biblical principles for extraordinary
leadership, business and politics.
Availability: Amazon & Kindle
Link to View: http://goo.gl/ecRMig

Title: Midnight Philosophies (E-book & Paperback)
Description: My Deep thoughts, Philosophies, Reflections –
Whispers of my mind.
Availability: Amazon & Kindle
Link to View: http://goo.gl/ecRMig

Title: This Godly Child of Mine (E-book & Paperback)

Description: A revelatory book on how to raise godly children
                    in a perverse and lawless world

Availability: Amazon & Kindle

Link to View: http://goo.gl/ecRMig

Title: The Deputy Minister for Corruption (E-book &
                    Paperback)

Description: A Novel

Availability: Amazon & Kindle

Link to View: http://goo.gl/ecRMig

Title: A Dove in the Storm (E-book & Paperback)

Description: A Novel

Availability: Amazon & Kindle

Link to View: http://goo.gl/ecRMig

Title: 100% JOB INTERVIEW SUCCESS
                    (E-book & Paperback)

Description: A simple, straightforward guide to passing
                    every job interview you attend.

Availability: Amazon & Kindle

Link to View: http://goo.gl/ecRMig

Title: Bible-by-Heart (Mobile App)

Description: A simple but effective App to help anyone
                    memorize 500 Bible verses in a year.

Availability: iTunes & Google Play Stores

Link to View: http://goo.gl/T3UdPN (i-Tunes)

Link to View: http://goo.gl/ljnECR (Android)

Title: Holy Rat (Mobile Game)

Description: An exciting Christian mobile game that
unwittingly gets you addicted to the word.

Availability: iTunes & Google Play Stores

Link to View: http://goo.gl/bygjBi (i-Tunes)

Link to View: http://goo.gl/F18RMO (Android)

ABOUT THE AUTHOR

Marricke Kofi Gane, is a gifted African Author, Philosopher, Public Speaker, Coach and Educationist. His writings carry real depth, are highly motivating yet challenging every status quo. He displays dexterity of mind and refined humour where appropriate. He is never shy in some of his works, to show a strong balance between his Christian roots and the reality of living in today's world.

Discover for yourself, all that his writings stand for - to dare, to motivate, to impact!! For more on him, visit www.marrickekofigane.com

Dear Reader,

Thank you for reading this book. I am hopeful that the information provided in it has given you some new learning, challenged you, or provided some answers and inspiration.

I respectfully ask your indulgence in 2 simple ways:

1. Whatever positive action(s) this book has inspired you to take, DO IT NOW. Not later.

2. Help other potential readers who without you, may never read this book by simply following the link below to leave a review. It only takes 3 minutes, but it could be a lifetime blessing for someone out there.

   http://goo.gl/v03bu2

Thank you once again for everything

Marricke Kofi GANE

53155845R00039

Made in the USA
San Bernardino, CA
07 September 2017